Gardening Leave is a rallying cry for change and an elegy to the hard nobility of the working men and women who poured our foundations and raised our walls; it is the work of a true artist, striving to smash forever "the chains that constrain us." The poet is democratic in his giving of voice: the 'ordinary', the outcast, the contingent, the forgotten, the abused, all sing from his lines. He gives voice to a bicycle. He gives living, sonorous voice to the dead. This is lifting, saving poetry, music for the heart.

— *Donal Ryan, Author*

In his highly anticipated debut collection, Eoin Devereux's robustly lyrical poems pierce through bourgeois pieties and restore to history those on the margins who have been unfairly overlooked. The poet explores the psychogeography of the quotidian, evoking the streets and arteries of childhood, the people who made an indelible impression. A beautifully poised book.

— *Emily Cullen,*
Meskell UL Poet in Residence

Eoin Devereux's poems rise up because they are born in real fires of memory and reflection, and because they contain a vital understanding of inequality. His narratives blend a deep retrieval of lived experience with a non-conformist commitment to questioning and casting light. A gift for every reader.

— *Martin Dyer, Poet*

BY THE SAME AUTHOR

David Bowie: Critical Perspectives (Co-Editor)

Morrissey: Fandom, Representations and Identities (Co-Editor)

Always Different, Always The Same: Critical Essays on The Fall (Co-Editor)

GARDENING LEAVE

new and collected poems

Eoin Devereux

451
Editions

Gardening Leave – new and collected poems
Published by 451 Editions, Dublin
www.451Editions.com

© Eoin Devereux, 2025

ISBN: 978-1-0684189-0-7

This book is sold subject to the condition that it shall not, by way of trade or otherwise, be lent, resold, hired out, digitally reproduced or otherwise circulated without the publisher's prior consent in any form of binding, cover, audio or digital format other than that in which it is published and without a similar condition being imposed on the subsequent purchaser.

Without in any way limiting the author's (and publisher's) exclusive rights under copyright, any use of this publication to "train" generative artificial intelligence (AI) technologies to generate text is expressly prohibited, as per Directive 2019/790 of the European Parliament and of the Council, 17 April 2019.

Cover image from AdobeStock.com/YONG

DEDICATION

for Liz, always

DEDICATION

for Liz, always

TABLE OF CONTENTS

ONE

Penny Boy	13
The Bullfield	16
All Belonging	18
Ordnance Survey	20
Moore's Road	24
Hawthorn	27
Owning Up	28
Lessons 1, 2 & 3	30

TWO

Blue Suede Shoes	35
A Different Rhythm	37
Panthera	38
Inside The Palace	41
The Cherished	43
Hidden Injuries	44
The Long Can	46
Murder In The University	48
Stranger Danger	50
Cribbing	52
Foxes	54

THREE

Francie Murphy	59
Pravda	61
Interior Weather	63
Laughing At The Moon	65
Carnivals	67

FOUR

The Bodhi Tree	71
A Garden Widow	72
In The Callows	73
Chitting	74

FIVE

Dublin 2	79
Revolutions	81
The Anchor Man	83
Duplicate(s)	84
Alice Murphy	86
A Letter From The Heart	88
A Steady Hand	89
Epiphany	91
Remnants	92
Swimming In The Rain	94
Hurdy Gurdy	95
The Foal	96

SIX

RSVP	99
Gavel	100
The Brace Position	101
Lindaville	103
The Trolley Collector	104
Trespass	106
High Tide	107
That Poetry Thing	108

Acknowledgements 113
Bio 114

ONE

PENNY BOY

At first,
my untutored
lazy eye
didn't even register
the many clues
scattered
all over,
the greasy streets of
this Pigtown.

From the wrong side
of the tracks,
we were shunted,
from the very start.
Our final destinations
pre-ordained
by Christian Brothers,
who routed us
to trades, labouring or the boat.

Classes called after saints,
harbingers of our
final destinations.

Patrick's,
Gerard's,
Nessan's,
Kevin's,
Malachy's,
Senan's.

Jim Kemmy and Johnny Rotten
helped me unpick the code.
My class honoured
the patron saint
of the falsely accused.
But that didn't stop
the dandruff and chalk-flecked teachers
promising to follow
our careers,
through Anco
or, better still,
the courts.

There were further hints
beyond the high walls of the school.
Fragrant Laurel Hill girls,
the well turned-out daughters
of the new monied,
who wouldn't dream
of telling their mothers
what part of the city

we hailed from.
Or the Mohair suited manager,
Who swiftly turned down
my softly spoken
job application,
to work as a Penny Boy,
in the Harrods of Limerick,
saying, they couldn't have
the likes of me,
knocking around
the finest emporium in town.

And for all the guff
about Doctors and Dockers
singing from the same hymn sheet,
the great and the decent
indelibly marked us.
Like the Children of Cain,
the stains went far deeper
than an Indian Ink dot.
We were forever judged
by estate,
street,
and accent.

THE BULLFIELD

On All Souls' Day
I knelt down on the mottled Tundra clay.
Ear cupped to the frozen ground,
I could faintly hear
the murmurings of men
buried, nameless in the paupers' grave.

Simple men like Francie Murphy and Brendan Plunkett,
let out for the day,
to belly crawl over damp drills,
handpicking potatoes, Greyhound Cabbage,
carrots, turnips, mangles.
It takes a lot of work to feed a hospital.

In the Bullfield,
I see Mattie Keane and Pa O'Brien,
able-bodied innocents,
chopping wood or ricking turf,
thrown the odd Players or Woodbine
as payment for their toil.

In the Bullfield,
I also see tormented men like Jim Sullivan and Dinny Ryan,
fattening pigs with sour milk and potato skins,
slopping out greeny brown scutter from their pens.
I see them all, and somehow cannot deny them,
men who were dumped in silence at first light,
from the back of a blue Ford tractor,
exchanging their labour,
for bed and board,
in the madhouse, named after
the Patron Saint of Workers.

ALL BELONGING

After four years
scrubbing floors in Brooklyn,
Brigid O'Sullivan returned
to sell root vegetables,
from a sturdy oak table,
placed across her front door,
near Stony Thursday Corner.

Cloaked in all weathers,
with just two Ranks' flour bags
loosely stitched together,
Dominic Kennedy,
a stocky car man,
carried heavy loads from Limerick Docks.
Having a gift with animals from his earliest years,
he stabled horses for Undertaker, Joseph Cross,
and ferried the city's poor and destitute,
to their final place of rest.

A factory hand,
from Carley's Bridge,
headstrong, Annie Gray
gulled the Wexford Constabulary.
She conveyed guns and bullets

secreted in the folds
of her Robin-Starched petticoats,
across the sloping town of Enniscorthy.

From Salt House Lane,
Eugene Devereux,
was the son of a Lime Burner.
The noble trade of cycle mechanic,
his initial calling,
he fashioned bicycles for five and three,
and was imprisoned for half a year
in rat-infested Frongoch,
having fought
for the new Republic.

All belonging to me
came from the land,
all belonging to me
worked with their hands.
My mother Anne, an assistant bookbinder,
my father Eamon, a chargehand fitter.

All made me, who I am.

ORDNANCE SURVEY, 1974

With neither map nor compass,
Ordnance House, Newtown Mahon
is my starting point,
as I traipse the street
of the mad,
the dead,
and the bad.

At the pitch-pine gates of Shaw's bloody slaughterhouse,
the sweet and sour smell of pig-shit
wafts over the squeals of terror,
the siren beckons clogged pork butchers,
sharpening their knives of steel,
to carve the finest cuts of ham and bacon,
for the bone china plates of the well-heeled,
while the city's poor devour the entrails of swine.

Under the watchtower of the jail,
in front of its needle-pointed railings,
my first salute is from a dancing, tweed-coated, toothless man,
'Well boss?' he says, as he waltzes alone.
His name is Raymond Troy,
but known, to all, since the day he was born,
as Bisto.

Caruso arms outstretched,
he sways, and sings a ballad of his own making:

'This street was named after the Lord Lieutenant,
he visited, just once, when we'd landlords and tenants,
the son of a Tory, he became a Whig,
this majestic boulevard's famous for the pig.
A writer and Dandy by temperament,
too honest for politics,
they say he was the last of the true romantics.'
'Oh Normanby's street has everything,
markets to sell butter and hay,
a battery, to keep the natives at bay,
a cobbled yard to drill young men,
sent out to die for Empire and King.
It has Early Houses for the thirsty and loveless,
a boot factory for the shoeless,
a jail to punish the poor,
a tea importer, a headstone maker,
a dusty flour mill for the baker,
a rope-walk for making a noose,
a fair-green with frisky horses and wild cattle on the loose,
a mad house, if you're not right in the head,
a spacious graveyard for when you're dead.'

The whole town knows Bisto,
he drank a spinster aunt's farm,
40 good acres, with frontage, near Ballybricken;
in the rats from drink, but well enough,

to be let out each morning from the lunatic asylum.
In his surgeon's hand, this singing, waltzing, Pierrot,
clenches a crumpled paper twist
to cargo coins of silver and copper,
when he heads to Mousey Delaney,
the blind huxter.

Bisto's scribbled list doesn't vary much,
a golden pimple necked quart of Lucozade,
for poor demented Jackie Stritch,
a few loose Player's for Mad Mary,
The Examiner for Fr. Tom Tracey,
a bar of Fry's for Jimmy Morrissey,
hairclips and rouge for Michael The Lady.

When his errands are complete,
Bisto will return to Josephs,
where strait-jacketed time
is counted by the asylum's four faced clock.
The days of ice-cold baths are long gone,
banished, like the all-seeing eyes of the Governor's panopticon,
in these more enlightened days,
the tormented are treated with wonder drugs,
talk therapy and ECT.

I continue my stroll,
nodding at a few more familiar faces,
broken men and women, whose countenances
are marked with the crows' feet of poverty.
I pass the gaunt Victorian villas,

on the left-hand side of the street.
Boru House is my next stop, constructed in 1880, A.D.
A lofty, red-bricked house,
built for a horse-dealer, with notions,
just last week, an obituary in *The Times of London* revealed,
that his famous, writer daughter, was sadly; deceased.

Two hundred yards up the street, just across from the Pike,
the Fair Green wall is beginning to crumble,
white, hand-painted words boldly proclaim:

'Kemmy For The Council.'
I first heard of Big Jim at my grandmother's funeral,
under a black mantilla, a pillar of the community asked:
'What's that fucking Communist doing here?'
the solid stonemason stayed at the back of the cathedral,
quietly paying his respects.

I cross the forked road, continuing on my way.
My quarry, this August morning, is to find
the final resting place of
Ellen Sharkey.
Aged 53 in 1855, Ellen was the very first to be placed
under the stony loamy soil at Spital Land, location 90a.
For six years, the wealthy of the town
refused to be buried,
alongside the poor, starving and demented.
This was finally resolved by creating
separate quarters for the poor and the quality.

Who says death has no hierarchy?

MOORE'S ROAD

Three narrow chimney stacks
watched over Moore's Road,
the smallest of them stunted,
because it took up smoking,
when it was young.

During a lunchtime swim
a migrant salmon was caught
by putting salt on its tail,
in the dusty world of the fitting shop
pheasants, rabbits, cooking apples
were often exchanged.

One foggy Saturday,
in Cooper Hill,
we climbed heaven-wards
into the steeple-high crane.
Anchored, on a pontoon,
it dredged grey mud
from the river's edge,
for the making
of Portland Cement.

The trick to climbing, you said
is to never look down.

Some years later,
when the Danish Bosses were long gone,
the factory offered a quarter of an acre
to its loyal workers
for a token penny a year.

To find the place,
you entered through a gap
in the bramble ditch on Moore's Road,
where endless potato drills
were weeded
by our calloused townie hands.

The secret, you said
is to work at a steady pace.

It was a strange place to be
at the age of fifteen
caught between rural roots
and the guff of punk bravado.
'Ashes to Ashes'
brought me to a different place,
courtesy of the Pye transistor radio,
stooped over mounds of wet late August mud,
hand-picking potatoes.

He's a quare hawk, you said
- Bowie - the scary British Queen.
The allotments lasted only a few years,
they were ploughed over
to make way for other kinds of plots,
a new cemetery
to bury the expanding city's dead.

And when it was time,
for you to leave the factory behind,
you did not once look over
your broad shoulders.

There's a knack to surviving, you said
it's to never look back.

HAWTHORN

At the end of our terrace,
there was a triangle of rough ground,
just big enough for a small bonefire
or an ancient funeral mound.
In its centre,
a stunted Hawthorn
bruised,
calloused,
deformed.

OWNING UP

My grown-up sons
cannot control their laughter
when they hear
my passionate proclamation,
that I still consider myself
Working Class.

Our conversation is governed
by rules unspoken.
It travels an expanse
of well-trodden ground.

On the debit side:	On the credit side:
my current address,	my council estate upbringing,
salary,	my family's history,
change of accent,	my activism
my social mobility.	my inverted snobbery.

In the end,
it's the older of the two
who has the last word.
Trying to keep a straight face,
he says:

Jesus, Dad,
next, you'll be saying
you're still
a Socialist.

LESSONS 1, 2 & 3

1.
When our homework
was a blind man's map
we were dispatched for
Pink Paraffin,
the evening newspaper,
or an oven fresh loaf.
On returning,
she'd always say,
don't mind your teachers,
those lessons
will sink in.

2.
She gave us
words
never seen
in school primers
or newspapers:
Randyboo,
Haboo,
Streel,
Gabhail,
Gohack,

Gaatch,
Fooster,
Grawvar,
Grig,
Kippins,
Faireen,
Pilgarlick,
Mee-aw
Tilly,
and,
best of all
Doll-dydee.

3.
She taught us
lessons of her own:
pray to St Anthony,
he's a great man for finding lost things,
respect all sacred places,
churches, stone circles, fairy rings.
Gather mushrooms,
before the rising Sun
scorches the tears

of glistening dew.
Never pick blackberries
after a shower of rain,
and never pick sloes
at the back of Halloween.
Look neither up to
nor down
on anyone.
Pedestals
are for statues,
not people.

TWO

TWO

BLUE SUEDE SHOES

Remembering,
can be a perilous thing.
In heavy November rain,
when rotten leaves, twigs and fag butts
clog the drains,
I see my father's face
in petrol rainbow-stained puddles.
He is young,
kind, Brylcreem quiffed,
not yet given to violence.
He's in the galley kitchen
of our motherless house,
beer merry,
singing about shoes.

Brushes of lustrous horsehair
and a ragged sock
are taken with gentle care
from his Box of Tricks.
The Box lives under the sink.

As he works, he croons:
'One, for the polish,
Two, for the shine,
plenty of elbow grease,

lots of spit and
they'll be fine
but don't you… step
on my Blue Suede Shoes…'

He waxes and scrubs,
waxes and rubs,
caressing each shoe,
as if they were pieces
of wafer-thin
Chinese Porcelain,
and when he finishes,
he tenderly places them
on the narrow kitchen table,
to sit and wait
on pages ripped
from Friday's *Irish Press*,
five pairs,
all black,
lined up
for early
Sunday Mass.

A DIFFERENT RHYTHM

Night-time brings
a different rhythm.
I check my possessions,
my transistor radio,
my tattered *Catcher In The Rye*,
a creased and cracked family photo.
I place my last fiver in my right shoe,
and turn away from the traffic's searching lights.
Zipping up my sleeping bag,
I check my possessions
a second time,
a third time,
a fourth time.
My headphones block out the noise.
I shut my eyes,
hoping,
to be lulled
to sleep
by the static
between the stations,
hoping to survive,
the night.

PANTHERA

Just eight winters old,
Hope, my daughter, is sleepless
because of the din
seeping through the floorboards
of tonight's resting place,
a snug hotel room,
big enough to swing
an anorexic Tom Cat in.

She says: 'Tell me a story Mam, from when you were small.'

I put down my click clacking needles
to weave a yarn she's heard before,
rehearsing a threadbare tale
concerning my very first storybook
and the cold, but dry, daffodiled February day
I first held it in my Lilliput hands.

'How did you pay for it?'

Everyday, for one whole year
I saved and saved,
eight fistfuls of dirty coppers.
I planked them in a jam-jar
in the always night cubbyhole
under the stairs.

I handed them over
to the stout grey cardiganed assistant
in that big bookshop
by the bus stop in town,
He counted them out,
one by one.

'And you could barely see over the counter…'

Yes, I was short legged for my age,
but that didn't stop me from racing home,
leaping across streets, lanes, rows and bows
to devour the strange words,
and savour the wild pictures
scattered across the Savannah
of every single page,
whilst dangling my feet
from the third step
of the linoed stairs.

'What was it called and what was it all about?'

THE BRAVE INDIAN LION
He lived in the Gir Forest
under the shade of a Banyan Tree.
Short of mane, he was known to all, far and near

for his caring nature, his wisdom and kindness,
especially to those who were weaker than him.

'Did he help people like us?'

Oh, he really cared for people like us,
the roofless,
the faceless,
the voiceless.

He lifted people who'd fallen,
he minded people who were broken,
he fed people who were hungry,
he calmed people who were angry,
he was a very brave Lion,
in the face of all adversity.

My worry-stone words reassure,
and, for now, the questions cease
despite the Party-Political Conference noise
underneath our Emergency Accommodation resting place,
Hope, drifts into a safe harbour of sleep.

INSIDE THE PALACE

Pasolini was right.
Inside the palace,
No one cares.

No one cares,
for the carers,
for the sofa-surfing,
for the working poor,
for mothers queuing for food parcels,
or the families imprisoned
in cheap hotels.

Inside the palace,
no one cares,
for those sleeping in doorways,
under bridges, in skips, in cars,
for those locked up in Direct Provision
or sheltering in LIDL tents,
in the Phoenix Park.

Inside the palace,
no one cares,
for the smack heads,
crack heads,
teenagers on Benzos,
or children banished into Social Care.

Inside the palace,
there is a grand coalition:
Bailed Out Banks,
Multinational Corporations,
Vulture Funds,
Landlords,
Gated Communities,
Payers of the minimum wage,
Janus-faced politicians,
the We All Partied Brigade.
And don't forget the social scientists
expressing their heartfelt concern
while requesting samples of spit
to ascertain if the unemployed
experience more or less stress;
or the journalists
who parachute in
to scribble their annual staple,
reassuring those inside the palace
that even the homeless
are granted a place,
for one night only,
at the Christmas table.

Pasolini was right.
Inside the palace,
no one cares.

THE CHERISHED

Young mothers of three on welfare
living on no-go sink estates
named after revolutionary leaders.
Out of work broken-spirited fathers,
Travellers trailered in Third World squalor.
Invisible rough sleepers,
displaced Asylum Seekers,
incarcerated teenagers,
terrified A & E stretchered elders,
madmen released into community care.
Zombies,
on heroin,
methadone,
crack cocaine.
Battered girls and women
down laneways turning tricks,
to pay for their next fix.
All are free from the foreign oppressor,
and all are cherished equally.

HIDDEN INJURIES

Fianna Fáil,
Fine Gael,
The Labour Party,
entrepreneurs,
risk-takers,
captains of industry,
the Squeezed Middle,
and Jesus Christ, worse still,
expert working groups,
consultants,
acronym creators,
golf players,
auctioneers,
property developers,
middle managers,
Green Jersey wearers,
drivers
of our small open economy,
never
refer
to the C word,

never,
ever,
refer
to
the hidden injuries
of Class.

THE LONG CAN

The headlines
were silent
on the white-collar crimes of the rich,
mute on employers who underpaid.
No ink was ever wasted
to tell the story
of the girls
who scrubbed shit
from sheets and smalls.
Nothing at all
was written
about the older ones,
enslaved for life
to hand-craft
delicate gossamer lace.

Not a single word was said
About those Sundays
when the incarcerated faithful
entered the tiny church
through an underground tunnel
and sat in their own quarters;
or how the mothers amongst them
had to crane their necks

in an effort to see
their orphaned sons and daughters
queuing for communion.

Not a syllable was permitted
in chapel, workshop or laundry,
between those women and girls
and the town's devout citizenry.
Jailed without trial
in the Long Can,
their only crimes:
being poor,
being stupid,
or being a source
of temptation.

MURDER IN THE UNIVERSITY

In a memo to the Campus Community
the Chancellor
declared,
there will be a blanket ban
on poetry.
The Department of Sociology,
will no longer teach
Weber's Iron Cage of Bureaucracy.
Going forward,
class will not be discussed in class.
All students will be referred to as customers,
lectures will be replaced
with Learning Encounters.
All tutorials will be
commercially sponsored.
Tenured Professors
will be sacked and re-hired
in a new Academic Gig Economy.
A Committee for the Regulation of All Policies
(or CRAP for short)
will meet, bi-monthly.
A Sunset Task Force
of Industry Stakeholders
will be convened.

This is to ensure,
the Chancellor stated,
greater agility and flexibility,
after all, the economy
has to be our sole priority.
Somewhere between teaching
about repetition on The Fall's first LP,
and the 90 or so Yes's in Molly Bloom's Soliloquy,
a new order,
murdered
the university.

STRANGER/DANGER

The school-run chat
drifts across the pristine avenue of
this much sought-after estate.
It's the kind of place
where the residents colour co-ordinate
their designer Wax Jackets and Wellingtons
before rolling out
the correct Wheelie Bins
every other Monday night.
It's the type of place
where Golf Widows dream
Valium dreams
and children are reared
by Spanish or Brazilian au-pairs.
It's the sort of place
where the inhabitants share
fear struck WhatsApp chatter
about strangers
in their midst.
It doesn't matter who they are,
tarmacadam purveyors,
window cleaners,
gardeners,
line-sellers,

hoodie-wearers,
pyjama-wearers,
Travellers,
white van men,
someone is sure to message:

"All I know is, they are not from around here."

CRIBBING

To be perfectly honest with you
I knew exactly what I was doing
when I swapped places with the Baby Jesus
in the Pro Cathedral crib.
It was just before the sacristan
bolted the heavy oak doors
to shut out the cold, dark, unforgiving night.
I stepped over the low trellis,
and hid, between Mary and Joseph
and the herd of plaster cast animals.
The early faithful
discovered me before first mass.
They were horrified
to see a naked Black man
curled up on the hard,
straw strewn floor.
And I didn't kick or scream
when the arresting officer
shepherded me away
swaddled in a standard issue
Garda overcoat
(size 3 XL).
As he pushed me into the squad car
he muttered something about
my lot coming over here

freeloading,
being a burden
on the state,
taking our women
our houses,
our precious cribs,
and our jobs.
And, he said, when the lads inside
hear what you did
to the Baby Jesus
you'll get what's coming to you,
my bucko.
I've been called much worse
since arriving here,
and to be honest with you,
I didn't care.
A stretch in the Joy
held no fear,
at least, I'd have a bed
and somewhere to shelter
for the night.

FOXES

During her regular morning walk,
Mrs Flynn stopped
to warn me about Foxes.
They're coming out here, she said,
from those welfare estates in town,
throwing shapes,
drinking,
shifting,
spitting,
travelling by E-Scooter
bus, bicycle or stolen car.
And, she added,
I have it on good authority,
that their ringleader
is a guy called Ginger Hickey.

It's not just our designer chickens
de-luxe wheelie bins,
or bespoke angora rabbits
they're after.
Oh no.
My new Infra-Red doorbell camera
has captured them
casing houses,
checking windows, doors,
even our pristine 25-2 Tesla cars.

Shy Brian, in No 3, told me
that just last week,
two Todds, in designer black hoodies,
jumped a shop counter
demanding chicken rolls, cigarettes and cider.
Mrs Flynn, he said,
you should've seen
the go hack of them
with their blood red Docs,
fade cuts and bling.
And, Shy Brian from Number 3, added,
sometimes, Mrs Flynn
there are Vixens,
wearing nothing
but pyjamas,
false eye-lashes,
smothered in fake tan,
all the while,
suggestively shaking their BBLs.
It's like the Kardashians.

These Foxes,
Mrs Flynn warned,
are a serious threat
to our community.

We are the people
who get up early
in the morning,
and now there is talk
of more of them
coming here
from out foreign.
That will be even worse.
Those Foreign Foxes
haven't a word of English.
Something will have to be done
by someone.
We'll have to
gate the estate,
close the borders
remain vigilant,
or else
there'll be
anarchy,
a complete breakdown
of everything
we have worked for,
of everything
we hold
dear.

THREE

FRANCIE MURPHY

Early Spring,
butter-palmed
Francie Murphy, aged 54,
breaks solid ground.
Using his father's gravel sharpened spade,
he slices sods, loam, heavy clay.
Just nine inches down,
he unearths the scraggy remains
of an angry young man,
in a hurry.

Mid Summer,
green-kneed
Francie Murphy culls
bottle blonde scutch grass,
rhubarb doc leaves,
blow in weeds,
foot tall electric nettles,
bottle green rushes,
dandelions, ragwort,
nodding thistles.
In the luxuriant lazy beds,
egged on by rotting fronds
of Spring Tide seaweed,
Francie Murphy plays God,
choosing which leggy seedlings
to kill, with his bare hands.

Late Autumn,
stout-bellied,
from his marriage to porter,
Francie Murphy wears
his mother's sized seven Wellingtons.
He takes treacle steps over nineteen and a half damp acres,
and plucks the last blackberries and hazelnuts
from brazen hedges, already hoary
with mildew, frost and Puca spit.
These are small fields reclaimed by his father's father,
each of them named, as you would, a newly baptized child.
In this world, fields are more important than love.

In the grey light
of the hardest of Winters,
just three weeks short of reaching
half a century, plus five,
Francie Murphy stands
by the ox-blood barn door.
A cincture of rope
secures his three coats.
He stews on the bones of his life,
with no one,
but a mongrel bitch
for company.

PRAVDA

(i.m. Sean Bourke)

My cousin Desmond, a versifier
worked for Ezra Pound,
my uncle Feathery, a rich miser,
gave pennies for scrap
in tumbledown
Limerick Town.

I served my time
as a banana stealer;
a bomb maker;
a jail breaker;
a scribbler.

I taught myself in Wormwood Scrubs,
I forgot myself in Moscow pubs.
Seduced by whiskey;
repulsed by poverty;
I was a reluctant guest
of the KGB.

The hard lessons I learned
came not from Christian Brothers
nor Daingean Industrial School,

and I realised, a long time ago
that Richard Lovelace was no fool.
Stone walls do not corral;
cages do not contain;
the chains that constrain
us most of all,
often spring from within.

INTERIOR WEATHER

On Doldrum days
no words flow,
I borrow
a jet black mongrel
from a stout man camping near the Pollack Holes.
The dog and I take the salty air,
tramping our Stygian way
to Newfoundout,
George's Head
or Byrnes' Cove.

On Doldrum nights
in my rattling wind whipped caravan,
perched near the Percy French Estate,
I sing and raise my only glass to ghost voices,
pinched jailed faces from Daingean and Wormwood Scrubs;
scribblers who once visited this coastal town:
Che Guevara,
Charlotte Bronte,
and Alfred Lord Tennyson.

On brighter days,
overcoated and bunkered,
I batter a pawned typewriter
in a shelter of cement grey.

Facing the calm sea,
as the gulls slowdive,
in search of prey,
I hammer out
2,000 words a day,
remembering,
Mike Randle
and Pat Pottle,
my latest exegesis
revealing
dark secrets
of MI6
and the KGB.

LAUGHING AT THE MOON

In this town
they call me
Mad Mikey,
Mikey Monday's
or, more simply,
Moon.

They call me Moon
because my mother
prayed to Luna
in vain hope
of an easy birth.
Sign is on.

Sentried at street corners,
I hear people mutter:
watch your man,
especially when
there's a full moon.
That's when his madness
comes into its own.

On moonlit nights,
poverty nuns
try to humour me,
offering tea, alms and sympathy.

Cidered teenagers scream
Tell me why, I don't like Mondays.
My stock reply is to gently croon,
By The Light of The Silvery Moon.
In truth, Selena has no power over me,
but, I have to work the crowd you see,
I fine tune my howls
as Luna rises and falls,
I know my place,
I never let my public down.

CARNIVALS

Eily Carty had it
that Alice Murphy died,
in her good armchair,
on the Tuesday,
after the Whit Weekend.
Having shunned her for years,
the pious of the town
turned out in their droves,
to the tiny funeral parlour
on Maudlin's Folly.
Good people all,
they cast their incantations,
mouthed robotic
Hail Marys and Our Fathers
in the balmy June air,
just days before,
the honeyed temptations of
the Strawberry Fair.

FOUR

THE BODHI TREE

We weren't that surprised
when Paddy Brassil pointed it out to us,
for he had a weather eye for such things.

A hazel tree sprouting in the left-hand corner
of our trim suburban tablecloth garden,
and, for all our weeding and trimming
spraying and mowing,
we'd never noticed it.

Paddy knew:
how to read clouds,
why a clamour of rooks would swoop in the evening air,
when there'd be a hard winter,
where the best wild mushrooms were.

He minded our tree, as if it were his own,
in early Spring, he heralded its new catkins,
in Summer, he peered through the green cloaked branches
to see if the house-sparrows had fashioned a home.
in Autumn, he harvested its tanned fruits, one by one.

He knew:
that we live just once,
that there is no such thing as Heaven,
that we all return
to the earth,
to begin the cycle again.

A GARDEN WIDOW

He's on Gardening Leave,
suspended with full pay.
And by Jesus, he's taken them at their word.
All he wants to do these days
is garden,
garden
and make fucking compost.
He has my heart broken.
And of course,
he never asks me
how I am.
It's all bin heat,
and the careful mixing
of carbon and nitrogen.
He talks non-stop
about the layering
of shredded cardboard
and grass cuttings
and sometimes about dying.
I'm married to a man
who pisses into the compost bin
once a week,
to speed up
the process
of decomposition.

IN THE CALLOWS

When sleep and joy
were scarce patterns
and words and singing
didn't come easily,
she picked Pissy Beds
pretending they were
the rarest of things.
She didn't give a whit
about her once nimble fingers
being burned
by Hogweed
Sumac
or Nettle stings.
In the Callows
she gathered
armfuls of Hemlock,
plucked hope
from Poison Ivy,
and dreamed
of better things.

CHITTING

In the season of forgetting
he set simple tests for himself.
In what order do the following
peep through the frozen marl and black clay?
Is it snowdrops first,
then tulips, crocuses or maybe daffodils?
When do the clocks change?
When is the next Leap Year?
Why is Easter not on a fixed date?
How do you make Whitewash,
Gooseberry Jam or Madeira Cake?
When is the best time to chit potatoes?

Snowdrops are the first arrivals.
Easter has to be a festival of light.
Whitewash, strangely, works best
if you add some blue dye.
Eggs for Madeira Cake should be left at room temperature
for two hours before you make your mixture.
Add some Elderflower Cordial to Gooseberry Jam
to guarantee extra sweetness and flavour.
In mid February put seed potatoes in an old egg tray
and place on a south facing windowsill.
Pinch out all of the potatoes' eyes, except one.

That will ensure a vigorous crop.

Sometimes,
in the season of forgetting
the answers drifted back
and sometimes, they did not.

FIVE

DUBLIN 2

Etched on the upright post,
underneath
my Brooks leather saddle,
a simple cypher tells
the place,
the week,
the month,
the year,
I was first assembled.
The alphanumeric code reveals
I was crafted
by Dublin hands,
in an Alpine roofed factory
where the Dodder kisses the Liffey,
at famed Hanover Quay.

Mouser Nolan from Inchicore,
indentured for just two years,
built my sturdy Raleigh frame.
When he was done,
Chargehand, Frankie Byrne
born and reared in nearby Ringsend,
added tyres of Indian Rubber
and a shiny Saint Christopher bell.

Pat Morrissey, a labouring man
from Irishtown,
pumped my tyres
oiled every crank, nut, bolt and moving part
before proudly wheeling me over Butt Bridge,
to Amien's Street Station.
Secured in the Guard's Van,
and dispatched on the evening goods train,
the sloping, sleepy town of Enniscorthy,
my final destination.

REVOLUTIONS

Liam Doyle bought me
from Eugene Devereux
Cycle Agent, Enniscorthy,
for five shillings a week
on the Never Never.
By trade, a miller,
I transported him at sunrise
to Davis's dusty flourmills,
and wheeled him home
in the evenings,
to lower Irish Street,
Via a thirsty detour.
I was chained to the railings,
while he met his friends
in Billy Stamp's fine establishment
on Market Square.

Some five years later
it was a small repair job,
– a slight tear on my Brooks Saddle –
that reunited cycle agent and miller.
Devereux recruited Doyle
to the Wexford 'A' Company
of The Irish Volunteers.

In April 1916
I played my part,
in the four-day revolution,
ferrying grub to the Atheneum,
carrying ammunition to the men
who took over Dodo Roche's Castle,
and the stumpy windmill on Vinegar Hill.

I escorted my owner to patrol
Scarrawalsh, Ferns, Oylegate, Ballycarney,
and with word of surrender,
back to his home in Irish Street,
Enniscorthy.

THE ANCHOR MAN

P.A. Crane took the snap,
Some seven weeks after the Emergency.
Three men sitting on
a strange looking bicycle,
a Triandum, on the footpath
outside the family shop.
At the rear, my grandfather,
steel-rod straight, commands the scene.
In the middle, my uncle,
dapper, smiling, suited and quiffed,
every bit the Hollywood star
you'd see on the Astor Screen.
Up front, my father,
holding the others steady,
looking ahead,
feet planted firmly
on the ground,
always
the anchor man.

DUPLICATE(S)

My father told me
I was named after
a whitesmith, who was out in '16.
Long before his revolutionary fervour,
he cycled his sturdy Humber
from Malin to Mizen,
and all parts,
in between.

My father told me
I was named after
a gunsmith, whose surgeon's hands
gently pruned telegraph wires
and blew railway lines to smithereens.
He and his comrades were
caged, without trial,
in a rat-infested distillery
in Frongoch,
Northwest Wales.

My father told me
I was named after
a locksmith, who duplicated
a key,

and secreted it
in a boiled fruit cake
thus allowing
Dev to escape,
from Lincoln Jail
in February, 1919.

ALICE MURPHY

I
am
invisibly inked
on the oily shop counter,
on the milk-washed terracotta tiles in the scullery,
on the snug linoed landing between attic and stairs,
on the gilt frame of the bloody Sacred Heart,
on the ivory keys of the upright piano,
bought for a song in 1944.
I can be found in the dusty curtain folds
of yellow gossamer,
and on the lampshade of creamy alabaster,
hanging forever
in the good room.

I
am
everywhere
in this three storied
Layer Cake house.

I
am
everywhere,

even though
Daddy
did not like
to speak
of such things.

I am everywhere.
I will always be here.

A LETTER FROM THE HEART

Every Monday,
before the porridge pot
was scrubbed and toast crumbs brushed away,
the City Edition was ironed,
rolled and entombed,
in a sheet of brown paper.
Addressed in finest copperplate,
entwined with a butcher's knot,
the squat parcel was sealed
with a red wax clot.

An S.A.G.
implored a safe passage
from postbox,
to mailboat,
to night-train.
The plea
to the Patron Saint of Lost Things
was not to protect
the tightly wrapped bundle,
but for the safe delivery
of the newsy epistle
secreted within.

A STEADY HAND

I built a wall
on a shallow foundation of sand and shale,
the largest boulders shouldering the greatest weight.
Guided by the batter-frame,
I layered mortar between the crevices,
firmly anchoring the Buck and Doe,
hearting the stone.

To break and shape the rock,
I used my father's 2 lb hammer
and his well-worn chisel of cold steel.
The steady staccato rhythm carried gravelly
echoes of his Player's Navy Cut voice.
In the hammer's ringing I heard him say:
'Four parts sand and one part cement
will give you the best mix.
Not too much water now,
…you don't want it too wet
and never too dry.'
Then he offered,
'All the tools in the world are fine, lad,
but what you really need for a job like this
is a steady hand and a keen eye.'

It's not just walls that protect us.
There's comfort in the traces
that people leave behind
and in our conversations
with them
when they're gone.

EPIPHANY

Early every October
she freed us from school
for a day's picking.
As we filled our jars and pails,
she'd retell the tale
of how, in that very field
Lómán was cursed
for refusing
to feed a team
of hungry jugglers.
We didn't know it then,
but the knowledge given
was as much
in the telling,
as it was
in the epiphany.

REMNANTS

On the day he was buried,
her friends and family said
it'll get easier,
once you are over,
the first Christmas,
the first birthday,
the first year.
Twelve months to the day,
she tackled the wardrobe and drawers
on his side of the room, packing away,
the Dunnes' Stores polyester ties, shirts, jumpers,
his good jacket, bought in Leonard's,
Outfitters for Gentlemen and Their Sons.
She gently folded the patched trousers
handy, he had always said, for just hacking around.
She platooned the black plastic bags
in the long narrow hall,
the oil slick sacks shouldered each other
like drunken fat scarecrows,
waiting for collection.
One week later,
she gathered his dog-eared books,
and laid them gently in cardboard boxes.
The rows standing like cheap pine coffins,
queued for cremation.

When that job was done,
save for Maritana and The Lily of Killarney,
she offered the choice
of his precious 78s and LPs,
to the local gramophone circle.
Its committee picked and mixed,
sifted and sorted,
between McCormack, Caruso and Gigli,
and the dregs were donated to
his favourite charity,
The Sick and Indigent Roomkeeper's Society.
For a while, she wanted to believe,
that the giving away of things
would help her forget.
Instead, his trace was tattooed,
in the most unexpected of places.
He was with the bumpy men shuffling to bus stops,
clutching oilskin shopping bags,
he was in carvery queues
requesting no onions, but extra gravy,
he was with the garden tools left out
in a shower of unexpected Summer rain,
he was in a turn of phrase, or words mispronounced,
he was in the rapid wingflap of collar doves
that swooped into the back yard,
unannounced.

SWIMMING IN THE RAIN

She crossed the makeshift timber bridge
erected over the Blackwater each summer,
and climbed the steep sand dunes.
Bathing costumes, buckets, fishing rods and nets were strewn
on the sloping lawn.
Her father's black Humber
was propped against the chalet wall,
the Billy-Can for milk from Joe Keating's
hung on a rusty nail.
Her father said if you stand on the highest sand dune,
on a clear day, you can see Wales,
before imparting that the Charismatics are back,
speaking in tongues,
praising Jesus
and laying of hands under canvass.
That was on the same day,
her mother had taught her
how to bury her clothes in the sand.
Wrap them Swiss Roll tight
in your towel,
if you ever go swimming in the rain.

HURDY GURDY

Forged from scrap metal
on a slack night
in the Cement Factory,
it stood, in the middle
of our concreted back yard.
On the face of it,
its intended purpose
was the drying of clothes.
To my child's eye,
it was a totem,
a rusty Maypole,
a Hurdy Gurdy,
a buried helicopter,
whose whirring blades
threw a flicker
across our small sitting room.
Green fingered
from an early age,
I planted my dreams
in tidy rows
underneath,
its spinning
shadows.

THE FOAL

Robbed of sleep, I watched a foal come into the world.
The Titian mare nuzzled and licked her oil slicked last born,
as if he were her first.

In the shadows of the wind lashed Hawthorn,
he rose, gingerly,
to stand
on his own.

SIX

RSVP

When Stockholm telegrammed
with the catastrophic news of a prize,
Samuel Beckett hid in the Riadh Hotel
on the rainswept coast,
at Nabeul.
He weighed up the cons and pros
of whether he should stay or go.
In the deserted milky twilight,
facing down
the engulfing
black waves of fame,
it dawned on him to suggest
that Jérôme Lindon,
might go in his stead.
His loyal friend
and publisher
would face the turnips,
at the august
December
ceremony.

GAVEL

From a rough slanted field
a streel of a scarecrow
bears witness.
A brimful cup on the doorstep,
an extra place at the kitchen table,
an empty chair by the fire,
a crossed, still-warm, loaf
on the slender windowsill.
Offerings to lost souls
who sometimes pass
in the night,
straying,
between here and there.

Darkness drops early,
in these quarter days,
but, the flickering of the Bonefire
permits her to see,
the masked mummers,
who traipse
from door to door,
clown-making,
seeking gavel.

THE BRACE POSITION

(for Liz)

Some five miles out from Rinneana,
the meeting place of the birds,
the passengers around me,
in Rows 34 to 38 (Economy)
were strangely silent,
when the captain calmly announced
an emergency landing
might be necessary.

I'd always imagined,
in situations like these
there'd be screaming,
prayers and tears.

The plane banked seawards
disgorging fuel,
killing time,
gliding over the Aran Islands,
over Liscannor Bay.
Back at base,
the fire crews readied themselves
with water and foam,
at the cusp of the poured concrete runway.

The unflappable air stewards
calmly demonstrated
the Brace Position.
Shoes discarded,
and heads bowed,
we dutifully rehearsed
our crash landing,
noting the strip lighting
and nearest Emergency Door.

It was in this silence
that I thought about never seeing you again.
It was in this silence
that I thought about
the importance
of what is not said,
of how words and talk
sometimes fail to express,
that which is deeply felt.

LINDAVILLE

Across the road
from The Bullfield,
Farrells is a trim and tidy shop.
Its castellated walls
just a conker's throw
from Wallers' Well,
and the swaying
bountyful
Chestnut trees,
keeping watch,
at Lindaville.
Further up the hill
bow stringed
Meagher's Viaduct stretches
over the Permanent Way.
Fat aerosol graffiti
on its straked sides
declares:
Punk Rock,
H-Blocks,
Gotta Getaway,
Stiff Little Fingers,
Join the IRA.

THE TROLLEY COLLECTOR

I was uncoupling
a tangle of trolleys
in ALDI,
for one of our
irregular customers.
By way of gratitude,
she said,
I have something for you.
I half expected her
to reach into her
Bag for Life
and pull out
cardboard tokens
or cheap medallions.
I half expected her
to tell me to pray
to St. Joseph of Cupertino
or to offer sage advice on
tolerance, silence
and the need to listen.
Perhaps she was going
to gift me an A3 poster
declaring, 'This Too Will Pass'
It crossed my mind that

she was going to suggest
mindfulness.
Instead,
she spoke about
the inevitability
of being alone
of the need to get out,
of the need to go on,
before adding
there are,
just two questions:
What are you
prepared to do
for others each day?
What are you
prepared to give away?

TRESPASS

Darkening our door,
she lands brazenly on our hearth,
casting long shadows.

HIGH TIDE

Even the highest
tide rushes away from you
after it rises.

THAT POETRY THING

On the morning after
I gave a reading
to an Arts Centre audience of four,
a near neighbour
(probably a trainee accountant
or a university lecturer, without tenure)
asked if there is much money
to be made from that poetry thing?

Instead of my usual response
to such queries,
where I quadruple
my royalties and fees,
I heard myself replying:

I write,
to try and make sense
of experiences good and bad,
I write, to give voice to stories untold,
I write, in an effort to call things out,
I write, to try and imagine,
a better world.

– FIN –

ACKNOWLEDGEMENTS:

Earlier versions of some the poems included in this collection have been published and/or broadcast previously by *New Irish Writing, The Irish Times*; *The Irish Independent*; *April is The Cruellest Month Poetry Broadsheet* curated by Eoin Devereux (2022); *Vital Signs* edited by Martin Dyar (Poetry Ireland, 2022); *The HCE Review*; *Southwords*; *The Ogham Stone*; *The Old Limerick Journal*; Drawn To The Light Press; *The Stony Thursday Book*; *Boyne Berries*; *The Storms*; *Lit 202*; *Janus Literary Magazine*; *1916: An Anthology of Reactions* edited by John Liddy and Dominic Taylor (Limerick Writers' Centre, 2016); *Dreams: 50 Years of Creativity, Culture and Community at the University of Limerick* edited by Joseph O'Connor, Eoin Devereux and Sarah Moore (Irish Academic Press, 2023); The Bookshow RTE Radio 1, *100 Words, 100 Books* (The O'Brien Press, 2014). *Limerick Writers For Palestine* edited by El Reid Buckley and Ellen Dillon (2024); *Children of The Nation: An Anthology of Working Class Writing* edited by Jenny Farrell (Culture Matters, 2019); *Fevers of The Mind Poetry Showcase*; *The Honest Ulsterman*; The Poetry Programme RTE Radio 1; The Poetry Jukebox and Poetry As Commemoration (2023); Words Lightly Spoken Podcast; Eat The Storms Podcast and The Holding Cell Podcast.

BIO

A Professor of Cultural Sociology at the University of Limerick, Eoin Devereux leads the Creative Writers in The Community modules on UL's MA in Creative Writing. His academic work includes co-edited books on David Bowie, Morrissey, Joy Division and The Fall. Eoin is one half of the Post Punk duo Dopamine Fix.

Eoin's short fiction and poetry have been published by The Irish Times and broadcast by RTE Radio 1. 'The Bodhi Tree' was shortlisted for a Hennessy New Irish Writing Award for poetry in 2018. 'The Bullfield' features in the Poetry Ireland Anthology Vital Signs (2022) edited by Martin Dyar. 'Revolutions' was included in the Poetry Jukebox as part of the Centenary of Commemorations project led by Poetry Ireland. New Irish Writing published Eoin's poem 'Pravda' in April 2024. It was subsequently shortlisted for the 2024 An Post Irish Book Awards New Irish Writing, Best Poem Category.

Eoin has performed his work on Podcasts such as Eat the Storms and Poetry Ireland's Words Lightly Spoken. He has been published in numerous journals including *The Stony Thursday Book*, *Southwards*, *Janus Literary Magazine* and *The Poetry Bus*. In 2022, Eoin curated *April Is The Cruellest Month*, a broadsheet featuring work by Kerrie O'Brien, Emily Cullen, John Liddy, Denise Chaila and novelist Donal Ryan. *Gardening Leave* is his first collection of poetry.

451
Editions
www.451Editions.com

www.ingramcontent.com/pod-product-compliance
Lightning Source LLC
Chambersburg PA
CBHW011127070526
44584CB00028B/3809